did you miss me?

jon santucci

Col. 1:28-29

TATE PUBLISHING *& Enterprises*

 TATE PUBLISHING
& Enterprises

All Scripture taken from the Holy Bible, New International Version ®, Copyright © 1973, 1978, 1984 by International Bible Society. Used by permission of Zondervan Publishing House. All rights reserved.

Published in the United States of America

ISBN: 1–5988668–7–7
06.09.05

Acknowledgements

My gracious Savior, who allowed me to write the words that He dictated to me. I would be totally lost without you.

My loving wife Kerry, thank you for your unfailing support and patience. I never would have started writing without your encouragement.

My parents, who have supported me throughout—even when I first told them I was writing a book.

Kerry's mom and dad, you're my favorite editor and sounding board. This would be gibberish without you guys.

Pastor Tom, Pastor Tim, and the rest of my church family, thank you for everything. I am so blessed to have you in my life.

Beka, Burkett, Mike, Mr. H, and the rest of my 4th period class, thanks for being my first read.

Table of Contents

Foreword

Jon is a devoted husband, writer, pastor, teacher, and co-worker. His take on the characters in the Bible, who show God's character for us to learn from, is a breath of fresh air. Jon Santucci has an insight and discernment into why God has put what seems to most of us to be insignificant stories in the most significant book ever written. This book will open your eyes to stories that you may have skimmed over in the past and bring a new outlook to your future. In fact, it may even change the way you look at God's Word. We all know that little events that seemed meaningless can look like monumental happenings down the road. It's the heart of this writer that brings the heart of God to life in the pages you are about to read. You won't be able to put it down, because you won't want to miss a second chance to experience these stories of struggle, hope, love, and faith.

- Tim Williams
International speaker and recording artist

Abraham's Servant
Genesis 24

Abraham's servant, possibly Eliezer, had one of the most difficult tasks a master could give. He was asked to go to his master's homeland and find a wife for his son. Obviously trusted by Abraham, he went about his task with only one real idea as to how to do it: pray. And God greatly rewarded the servant by providing Rebekah—a woman whom he could have only dreamed of!

How exactly are you supposed to go about looking for a wife for someone else? Abraham's servant had to wonder what exactly his master was looking for. This really wasn't a situation where he could afford to mess up. Did Abraham want a blonde or a brunette? Does Isaac prefer tall or short, a good cook, someone who wants a big family? What in the world do they want? And how to know if it's the right girl or not? This was no simple search-and-find mission.

After a long journey, he arrived at the well outside of the town of Nahor. The well was a great waiting spot, since many young women would be coming to get water for their families. He was probably still very anxious and confused as to how to go about finding a wife for Isaac. It's difficult enough to find one for yourself! A small part of him probably wanted to just go away, go back home where it was easier. Another part of him desperately wanted to please Abraham and Isaac. After all, this was the same Isaac that he had watched his master long for—even when it seemed hopeless. Isaac had grown up literally in front of the servant's eyes, and to find him a wife was an honor.

He wasn't sure how to find her, though. Then it hit him—he could ask the same God that his master was always speaking to and about for help. Abraham's entire success was linked to his God, so why not ask for success in this case as well? Long before Solomon wrote in Proverbs 16:3, "Commit to the Lord whatever you do and your plans will succeed," Abraham's servant did that. In one of the truly great prayers in the Bible, he asked God for success and a clear sign that God would pick the right girl for him. The smartest decision that he could have made was to leave it up to God and just watch what happened. The sign he asked for was actually an extraordinary one. "May it be that when I say to a girl, 'Please let down your jar that I may have a drink,' and she says, 'Drink, and I'll water your camels too'—let her be the one you have chosen for your servant Isaac."[1]

The prayer is extraordinary because the task he was looking for the woman to do was extraordinary itself. Abraham's servant took 10 of Abraham's camels with him on the journey. John Maxwell, in his book,

Running With The Giants, figured that for a woman to water all of the servant's camels would take approximately two hours.[2] To give a stranger a drink at the well isn't much of a stretch, but to water a small herd of camels definitely is. And it was the woman who was going to offer to do that. That's the same as asking a 10-year old boy to clean his room and expecting him to respond by offering to vacuum and dust the entire house, wash the dishes, then mop the kitchen floor.

But the plan was actually quite simple. Since he had little direction as to the type of person, he would search for a girl who had attributes that Abraham put a lot of stock in. He looked for a woman with a servant's heart—someone who did more than she was asked to do simply because that was her nature. He knew this type of girl would be appealing to Abraham because it was probably the type of person that the servant was himself. The reason why he was the chief servant was probably not because he was a family friend, but because he truly had a servant's heart. He did what was asked of him and then some. Abraham appreciated that, and the servant knew his master would enjoy seeing a similar trait in a daughter-in-law.

Then Rebekah walks up. Actually, it wasn't *after* Abraham's servant was praying but rather *while* he was still praying. In mid-prayer, God was already providing the answer. Just as he prayed for a woman with a servant's heart, Rebekah revealed that she had one. It was as if she was listening as he prayed, because she said the same words that he'd asked God to let the woman say. Immediately, this servant knew that his search was over.

Abraham's servant reveals to us the wonder that prayer is. That indescribable, yet very taken-for-granted gift that allows us to speak to the King of the Universe. The servant found out that when we pray, God hears us. And when we ask for help or direction, He provides it. Even when it seems that the task is beyond our grasp, He's willing to help us. He wants the best for us—just as the servant wanted the best wife for Isaac—and will help us in that. But we have to ask. How long would the servant have been waiting if he'd never prayed about it? Just as James 4:2b says, "You do not have because you do not ask God."

Jonathan's Armor Bearer
I Samuel 13:23-14:14

Here's a nameless person who God used in amazing ways. Depending on your perspective, Jonathan's armor bearer is either very stupid or unexplainably bold and loyal. Jonathan was the son of King Saul. By this point, Saul had the Israelite army headed in a questionable direction as both they and the Philistines waited in a standoff. To make things worse, the only two people in the Israelite army that had weapons were Saul and his son. So Jonathan took things into his own hands—and he brought his armor bearer with him. And they took on 600 enemy soldiers. That little skirmish, along with a God-induced panic that swept throughout the Philistine camp, helped the Israelites rout their enemies. But Jonathan's armor bearer went a long way in making it happen.

Jonathan isn't best known for his military expertise, boldness, or for being the son of a king. Instead, he's best known for his close friendship with and loyalty to David. That trait of loyalty was clearly something that Jonathan also appreciated from others, and his armor bearer portrayed that to the full. So when Jonathan left the camp by himself, his armor bearer was close behind. And when Jonathan wanted to go to a Philistine camp to basically pick a fight, his armor bearer put up no objections. Maybe it was out of respect that he didn't say anything, maybe it was fear, or maybe it was an unbreakable trust.

The two of them stood there alone, looking up at the Philistines. It was probably pretty quiet. Jonathan looks intrigued; the armor bearer looks at Jonathan. As one ponders if attacking is God's will, the other watches and studies. Each is wondering what the other one is thinking—or what he himself is thinking for that matter. They're not really going to do this, are they? Jonathan broke the silence with an eerie line, "Come, let's go over to the outpost of those uncircumcised fellows. Perhaps the Lord will act on our behalf. Nothing can hinder the Lord from saving . . ."

The armor bearer couldn't help but say, "Do all that you have in mind. Go ahead; I am with you heart and soul."[3] He may have been motivated by Jonathan's words or have known that God was capable of anything. Maybe he just wanted to play Robin to Jonathan's Batman. Either way, the armor bearer completely went with the plan and didn't hold back. He could have said, "Yeah, right. I'll spot you from here. Tell me how it went." But he didn't. He went without objection or hesitation. The armor bearer had complete trust in Jonathan and the God that he believed in.

As the two of them revealed themselves to the Philistines, Jonathan told the armor bearer what the sign from the Lord would be. When the Philistines saw them, what was the armor bearer thinking? "Oh my goodness, there's a lot of them; I wish I stayed home." No, he was probably thinking, "Let's fight!" They got the sign they were waiting for and climbed up the cliff to the Philistine camp. Even though they were at a disadvantage from a militaristic standpoint, they had a major advantage considering that God was on their side.

The two of them teamed together to take on the Philistines. Literally fighting back-to-back, the two had complete faith in what God had promised them. Working together is something that God has always been pleased with. In Ecclesiastes, Solomon said that two are better than one. When Jesus sent out the 72, he sent them out in pairs; He did that so when one was discouraged, the other could be an encouragement. When one was timid, the other was fearless. And when the 72 came back, they were excited to tell Jesus all the success they had.

In a similar way, Jonathan and the armor bearer were successful by killing at least 20 of their enemies while coming out of the battle unscathed. And the armor bearer probably came down the cliff with a similar attitude to the one he had going up it. He just watched Jonathan, almost in awe of the man whom he faithfully served. He probably wondered where Jonathan's resolve and trust came from and felt thankful to know a man of his stature. And Jonathan probably came down completely thrilled to have such a loyal helper, realizing he would be dead without the armor bearer, knowing that none of this could have been accomplished alone.

We need to be more like the armor bearer, having a complete trust in what Jesus tells us to do. Even when the odds seem overwhelming, we need to know that God always has our best interests in mind. We need to know that no matter what the situation, just like the armor bearer, we'll come out of it unscathed and in awe of the God that we serve. Not only should we have complete trust in God, but also we can learn simple loyalty to the right friends. Our friends should know, as Jonathan did, that they have someone there to protect them and watch their backs. Someone who will go into battle with them if needed, always trusting where God leads, because some things that God calls us to can be better accomplished in pairs, rather than by ourselves.

Uzzah
II Samuel 6:1-7

The man is a mere footnote in the story of David bringing the Ark of the Covenant back to Jerusalem. And yet it's his action and God's response that are critical because they set an example for us. Not much is known of Uzzah, except that he was the son of Abinadab. Uzzah obviously had a good heart because he saw that the ark was slipping off the cart after the oxen stumbled and wanted to prevent it. Then it happened—God struck him dead. And in that moment of Uzzah's decision to touch the ark and his immediate death for it, we learn how to think.

The Ark of the Covenant symbolized God's promises to the people of Israel. It was stored in the Most Holy Place. It held the Ten Commandments, among other things. The ark itself was Holy. Just the mere presence of it was powerful and awesome. When the Philistines had it, they stored it in the temple of Dagon. The first night it was there, the idol fell on its face before the ark. It was put back up the next day, only for it to fall prostrate again—this time with the head and arms falling off. Wherever the ark went in enemy territory, the town was struck with horrific plagues of tumors and rats. The Philistines couldn't get rid of it soon enough.

Once the ark was brought back to Israel, it was kept at the house of Abinadab for 20 years. While Uzzah obviously never looked inside, which also would have instantly killed him, he understood what it stood for. He knew the power of the ark because his father's house had been blessed greatly during the time it was there. The ark, for Uzzah, clearly represented God's covenant with Israel as well as His amazing power and blessings. For him to be walking alongside the cart that carried the ark as the king celebrated and musicians played was a tremendous honor. This was the moment of his life. All were watching the ark being brought back to its rightful place in Jerusalem, and in the midst of the party is Uzzah.

What pride he must have felt! It didn't matter that King David was transporting the ark by cart instead of on poles carried by Levites as God had commanded in Leviticus. And if Uzzah did know the rules, who was he to tell the king that he was wrong? Besides, it couldn't be a big deal because such an amazing day couldn't be clouded by mere technicalities. This was a great day for the country. An entire generation had been born since the ark was in the Most Holy Place, and it finally was on its way home.

Then it happened. Maybe one of the oxen's hooves hit a stone and stumbled. Or possibly God just got infuriated at seeing the simplest of His laws carelessly broken. Either way, the oxen stumbled, and the ark—God's covenant and the pride of Israel—was starting to slip. Uzzah had a split second, maybe less. On one hand, since no man should be touching the ark, he could just let it fall. On the other hand, he could reach out and keep it from falling. How could God be mad at that? He was trying to preserve the ark that he had grown so fond of and which stood for so much. Keeping the ark in one piece had to reflect God's heart more than any old "rule," right?

And a second later, Uzzah lay dead. The music stopped. David fumed—at God. And God must have been disappointed. God wasn't disappointed because Uzzah was a bad guy, but because he didn't pay attention. Uzzah committed one of the easiest sins of all—justification. He justified a blatant sin by thinking that God would forgive him. After all, on the scale, letting the ark drop must have been worse than keeping it steady. But God doesn't work on some sliding scale; He lets us know His holy heart and tells us what pleases Him. And Uzzah's actions didn't.

First, we need to know God by spending time in His Word. It's very difficult to know what someone is feeling unless you ask, and God is the same way. To know the heart of the Father, we must seek it in the Bible. And once we know what He wants, we can't allow our own convoluted rationalizations get in the way of listening to and being obedient to God. If we know what's right in our hearts, our minds can't be allowed to convince us otherwise. Because sin, no matter what we want to call it, is sin. And since sin and God can't coexist, our choice should be simple. Often the right thing to do isn't the easy thing—or even the one that makes the most sense to us. But we do right because it pleases God, and pleasing God is what we're here to do.

Queen of Sheba
I Kings 11:1-14

The Queen of Sheba is one of those people you've heard of in the Bible but don't know much about. She was a queen, that much is known. She'd also heard many things from people about the wisdom of Solomon and wanted to know more. But instead of asking those who had met him or had second- or third-hand information about this genius, she decided to go straight to the source. And even after speaking with this king from a distant land, she realized that he was even better than advertised—a rarity, even then.

It was a long journey for the queen, about 1,200 miles to be exact. Probably on camel. Across terrain that wasn't exactly a paved road with rest stops every 25 miles or some sort of watering hole every other exit. It was a tough road trip for royalty to make. And while her servants went out of their way to make her as comfortable as possible, it was a pointless task. It was a long trip, it was a hot trip, and yet she chose to make it herself.

She wanted to do the examination herself. The queen had heard a great deal—as so many before her had—about the greatness and brilliance of this Israelite king. David was well-known, but more for his ingenuity and strength on the battlefield. Solomon was a different breed of king. He lived during times of peace, not war. He seemed to be blessed in every way: riches, livestock, women, etc. The rumors had become so great about Solomon that she had to know whether or not it was true. In fact, it was probably too good to be true.

As her caravan approached the palace, the queen caught herself with her mouth open on more than one occasion. She couldn't believe how amazing the kingdom was. Everything, down to the smallest detail, was better than others had said. As she walked into Solomon's throne room, the king was seated in his throne. He didn't look like some sort of fairy tale character, but rather a mere mortal. This couldn't be him, could it? His stature wasn't larger than life, and it wasn't like he had some sort of noticeable special powers of anything. He warmly welcomed her, and she sat near him.

She quickly got the pleasantries over with and immediately launched her barrage of riddles and questions at the wise king. He barely had to pause between the question and his response. Each answer was very poignant and bordered on amazing. She couldn't believe her ears. Nothing was too difficult or even challenging. It didn't take long for her to realize that he was no mere mortal as she had earlier surmised. He may, in fact, be mortal, but none could match his wisdom or candor. Her questions, no matter how puzzling, were answered in ways that a child could clearly understand. He was gifted. Her time with him was better than she could have hoped, and she left Israel better because of the time spent with Solomon.

Solomon may have been a genius, but his brilliance came from above. So when the Queen of Sheba asked her questions, it was as if she was getting answers straight from Heaven. But had she never gone, she would never have known. That's the same way we are with God. We often hear others speak of his greatness and blessings. We get some second- and third-hand testimonies of those He has miraculously helped, and we hope to someday know Him in the same way.

But unlike the Queen of Sheba, we never make the trip. While she was willing to endure more than 1,200 miles to hear a man speak, we fail to go 15 feet to read God's Word. She listened intently as he spoke, we fight our way through a 30-minute message once a week and only because we know that a brunch is waiting shortly after. She left amazed, and we leave puzzled— wondering where all these people get these stories of a great God. He doesn't reveal Himself to you.

Yes He does, but we need to make the effort. Solomon was there, waiting. The Queen of Sheba just had to make the effort, and she was richly rewarded for it. We don't want to discipline ourselves to get to know

God, so we end up missing Him completely. Instead of being blessed, we are frustrated by this mysterious God. He's no mystery, He's waiting. All you have to do is walk yourself into His throne room and take a seat close by. He'll take care of the rest.

Jeroboam
I Kings 11:26-12:33

There are so many kings listed in I and II Kings that it's simple to overlook some. Everyone knows David and Solomon; Ahab and Hezekiah are pretty well-known, while Josiah and some of the others are more than mere footnotes. Others are just on the list. Then there's Jeroboam, arguably one of the most influential of all the kings. As much as anyone in the Bible, we learn many key things about leadership from the life of Jeroboam.

His story is simple. Jeroboam was one of Solomon's officials who was tapped for greatness by Solomon himself. When he saw how well Jeroboam did with the tasks he was given, Solomon entrusted him with more. And God entrusted him with a great deal as well. Jeroboam was promised that he would be king over 10 of the tribes of Israel, and God went as far as to say that Jeroboam would start a dynasty equal to that of David's. All Jeroboam had to do was be obedient to God.

But once he was made king, Jeroboam lost sight of God's promises. He was willing to trade in obedience for his own pride. Having convinced himself that allowing his subjects to go to Jerusalem and worship as God required would cost him loyalty and eventually his life, Jeroboam flipped the switch. He created golden calves for the people to worship, telling them that they were the ones that had led the Hebrews out of Egypt. He only trusted God in what he could see and allowed his own humanity to trick him into sinning. He convinced himself that having the people sacrifice to altars, worship at shrines and be led by random "priests" would be alright. All these things broke God's heart, but Jeroboam figured it would be easier to do things his own way rather than obey God.

But not only did Jeroboam sin himself and lead the people away from God, he set a terrible example that was followed by many of the subsequent kings of Israel. Whenever the author of Kings would mention a new king, he would mention how the king lived and who he modeled himself after. Many of the kings of Israel patterned their leadership after Jeroboam. Ultimately, each man is responsible for his own life and will have to give an account to God for everything he did, but Jeroboam didn't just hurt his own relationship with God, he became a stumbling block for many who came after him.

David and Jeroboam were similar in that they were used as models, but they lived their lives completely opposite of each other. David was a man after God's own heart. He encouraged his son Solomon to be a wise king—the very trait that Solomon asked God to bless him with. Josiah followed God the way that David did and reformed the kingdom because of it. Jeroboam was selfish and pulled the people away from God for his own personal gain. He allowed his own insecurities to cloud his judgment and forgot that his eyes should have been on God and not on himself. He changed the kingdom drastically for the worse. He set the standard for men like Ahab and others to follow false gods and create their own rules. He deluded the people into thinking that God's way was an option and not a requirement in order to please Him.

It's crucially important to remember that people are watching us, even if we don't realize it. If somebody, anybody, finds a trait that they like in someone else, they will try to emulate it. Be it an athletic skill, style of dress, music they listen to, or an entire lifestyle, the world has always been a copycat society. The thought process is: "If it works for someone else, it could work me." And since the world thinks that way, the question is: What direction are we leading in? Paul understood this and often said that others should imitate him as he imitated Christ. Paul wrote in Philippians 4:9, "Whatever you have learned or received or heard from me, or seen in me—put into practice." Are we guiding others to Christ or pulling them away from Him?

Jeroboam missed the opportunity he had to guide

not only his contemporaries, but many generations to come toward God. Instead, he made it acceptable to wander from the Lord and what pleases him. Jeroboam gave the people alternatives to God instead of keeping the land pure for Him. He set into motion a model of evil, Godless leadership that would eventually be the downfall of the kingdom. Don't make the same mistakes that he did. Look for ways to be a positive influence, and don't allow yourself to get sidetracked from what pleases God. You never know what a godly lifestyle will mean to those who come after you.

The Whisper
I Kings 19:9-18

It's easy to miss—especially in light of all the other things that happen in these verses. Elijah, who was on Mt. Horeb, experienced three natural disasters before hearing a whisper and knowing that it was God. Something that was so quiet was so powerful! And in the midst of hunger and isolation and all the other frustrations that Elijah was enduring, it was the whisper that made it all clear. It probably wasn't how Elijah was expecting to hear from God, but it was the way that God chose to reveal Himself.

Prior to being on Mt. Horeb, Elijah had to believe that things were looking up. First, the miracle on Mt. Carmel happened, then the prophets of Baal were killed. Finally, the three long years of no rain or dew in Israel had ended. That meant no more hiding by a brook, no more wandering to find a poor widow with very little left. Things were going to be easier. Of course, Elijah didn't plan on Queen Jezebel vowing to kill him. He probably didn't plan on going another 40 days without food, either.

So God told Elijah to go up to Mt. Horeb. It was the same place that God first revealed Himself to Moses at the burning bush. It was known as the mountain of God. What better setting for Elijah to receive something amazing from God? So Elijah was told to stand on the mountain and wait for the presence of the Lord. And he did so, finding a cave in the mountain to wait in.

First, Elijah experienced a hurricane so strong that it could literally rip apart the rocks in a mountain. Even though Elijah knew he was waiting for God, you can imagine this prophet cowering in the corner of the cave waiting for the winds to die down. And once they did, Elijah was quiet, but God wasn't in the wind. Shortly after, an earthquake occurred. The very rocks that were loosed by the wind were now rumbling underneath him, and Elijah just tried to keep his balance in an area of the cave that appeared safe. Again he waited for God to reveal Himself—and again, nothing. Finally, a fire. He could feel the heat from the back of the cave and just prayed that rock was still not flammable. And once the flames subsided, Elijah had to believe that finally God would show Himself. That's the same way that He had revealed Himself to the people on Mount Carmel. But again, nothing.

After all of that, maybe an exhausted Elijah just lay down on the floor of the cave and exhaled. One natural disaster would be enough to slow down most people—to have three consecutively is unimaginable. Just as he started to relax, frustration also set in. If God was going to speak to him, why hadn't He done it yet?

How else would God reveal Himself if not through a hurricane, earthquake, or fire? That's how He works. Something major happens, and God is there, right? As Elijah ponders, he hears a voice. It's not very loud, so Elijah starts to walk out of the cave to get a better listen.

He knows the voice; it's the one he's been waiting to hear. Once Elijah leaves the cave, the voice is clear, but never gets loud. It's not booming or accompanied by fireworks, it's calm and quiet—a mere whisper. It's God. Speaking just as He promised He would, but maybe in a way that Elijah wasn't expecting. It was so simple.

A whisper is something very intimate. Physically, it's impossible to whisper unless the one speaking and the one (or ones) listening are close. And most people refuse to be physically close to someone they don't have a strong relationship with, meaning that whispering is something that involves trust on both ends. And when something is said in a whisper, it brings about an entirely different feeling. If a husband shouts, "I love you," to his wife, that's one thing. But when he holds her tight and lovingly whispers those same words, it's a totally different feeling.

So often we get confused about the way that God speaks. Understand, He can and will communicate however He pleases, but we are so obsessed with waiting for the loud, obvious shouts that we miss the inti-mate whispers. And those are so amazing that this should be our goal: To develop a strong enough rela-tionship with our Heavenly Father that we can hear those quiet words. That we can be so close to Him that He doesn't need to shout to get our attention. So the question is this: If God whispers, will you hear Him?

Shaphan
II Kings 22:6-11

Shaphan is one of those guys that got caught in the middle of something that he never anticipated. He was just going about his business, was handed something of great value, looked over it at least twice—and never realized what he had. Others knew exactly what it was and its importance, but Shaphan was completely oblivious. And because of this, he surely missed out on something that would have radically changed his life. It's not only that we miss Shaphan as we read the Bible, but we can learn from him because he missed God.

Shaphan was King Josiah's secretary who was sent to the temple to get and distribute the money that was collected. While he was there, Hilkiah, the high priest, seemed to be acting strangely. The two quickly took care of business, but it was pretty clear that something else was on Hilkiah's mind. The old man seemed anxious to tell Shaphan something. He finally said, "I have found the Book of the Law in the temple of the Lord."[4] The old man seemed excited, but Shaphan didn't completely understand why. What's the big deal about finding a scroll in the temple?

Hilkiah walked away to retrieve the document and came back with it cradled to his chest. He brushed it off one last time before carefully handing it to Shaphan. The high priest never moved; instead, he stood there with a quiet expectation that the king's secretary would greet it with the same enthusiasm he had. Maybe out of obligation, Shaphan began to slowly read it. The Book of the Law—either everything that Moses wrote (Genesis through Deuteronomy) or just Deuteronomy—contained the very words that God spoke. It captured those amazing moments between God and his servant Moses on Mt. Horeb, among other things. These words revealed the very heart of God, and Shaphan was reading it line by line.

It could have overwhelmed him, especially considering that the Law had been lost for so long. Or maybe, since the Israelites had wandered so far from God, finding the Law didn't faze him. Either way, Shaphan read the words and they were just . . . words. The Bible doesn't note anywhere that Shaphan was impacted by the Book of the Law in any way. Shaphan's lack of response is important, especially in comparison to the reaction that Josiah had. When Josiah heard the Law read to him, he was immediately broken. He tore his robes, a passionate sign of sorrow and guilt. It was the reaction of Mordecai when he heard that the Jews were condemned to die.

The Israelites weren't being sentenced to death in the Book of Law, but Josiah understood that the nation was breaking God's heart. Everything from the condition of the temple to the hearts of the people was far from what God desired. With each word, Josiah's eyes welled with tears. By the way, it was Shaphan that was reading the book to the king.

Twice Shaphan read the inspired words of God, and they didn't seem to affect him either time. Even when he told Josiah about the Book of the Law, all Shaphan could say was, "Hilkiah the priest has given me a book."[5] It was a, "By the way . . ." comment. Shaphan could have been thrilled, even humbled to be reading it for a second time. He could have burst in to see Josiah and barely contained himself as he read. Having never read the Book of the Law before, it could have been so touching that tears rolled from his eyes as he read—the type of thing where the words get blurry on the page.

But Shaphan couldn't cry, because the words had no impact. It's a situation in which we find ourselves all too often. We read the scriptures, which Paul reminded Timothy were "God-breathed,"[6] and we fail to realize that it's time with God Himself. We're in church hearing the Word being read, but we're not really listening. Many Christians have memorized John 1:1—"In the beginning was the Word and the Word was with God and the Word was God," but we don't treat it that way. More often than not, spending time in Scripture is the thing we are most creative in avoiding.

We've developed a nonchalant attitude toward the Gospel, the feeling that God's lucky if we spend time with Him, not realizing how much we miss out on when we don't. We would never want to be like Shaphan, but we are like him in more ways than we want to admit. It's something that we can change, though. Let's learn from Shaphan, not become more like him.

Jehoiada
II Chronicles 22:11-24:2

What an integral role this godly man played in the Old Testament, but very little attention is paid to him because of his supporting role in the life of King Joash. However, the reality is that Jehoiada was a major reason why Joash pleased God. II Chronicles 24:2 says, "Joash did right in the eyes of the Lord all the years Jehoiada the priest instructed him." Jehoiada took on the role of father, teacher, advisor, and protector to Joash, who became king when he was just seven years old. Not only was Jehoiada responsible for helping Joash rule over Judah, but also for training him to be a godly king.

On one hand, it sounds very appealing to be an advisor to a child-king because of the power that comes with it. On the other hand, Jehoiada was forced to change diapers and toilet train Joash, teach him to read and write, and go through the often tedious process of rearing someone else's child. Jehoiada did all of this knowing that if Athaliah found out, she would have him killed for treason. Athaliah was the mother of King Ahaziah. She killed off the royal family after her son died and ruled the land for six years. Jehoiada had very little to gain by raising Joash; he had everything to lose.

What better teacher to have, though, than the high priest. Jehoiada knew the heart of God and sought to live it out in his own life. Joash received formal instruction but also must have learned much by watching Jehoiada on a daily basis. Imagine what it was like for the child to be running around the temple, mimicking Jehoiada's every move, asking those "Why" questions that can be so very annoying, and receiving answers that were life changing. He heard from a young age about the building that was the dwelling place of the Almighty God. Imagine how much of an impact those talks had, constantly hearing the stories about Moses and the slaves in Egypt and tales of angry King Saul and the cunning young David. Jehoiada was able to explain the importance of each artifact in the temple and how each one related to the Holy One.

In a very short period of time, Jehoiada took on the tasks of protector, equipper, and judge. Jehoiada is, in a small way, a mirror of God Himself. But Jehoiada's legacy is being a godly and good advisor who did what was right, even when it was scary. Jehoiada's greatest individual moment came when Joash was seven and Jehoiada realized that it was the right time to take control back, giving it to the young king. He risked his own life and taught an unpopular theology, knowing that it should impact an entire kingdom. And he did it to see God, the one he served so faithfully for a lifetime, glorified and pleased through the life of the child.

God wants us to have the same attitude in our life that Jehoiada did. To make the effort to do what's right, even when it's unpopular, could cost us friendships, money, or whatever else we place in great importance. To care more about Him than anything else because it's all about Him! To take the time to impact the life of someone else, knowing that the Gospel is contagious and can spread like wildfire—it just needs a spark. The spark and love for the Lord that God used Jehoiada to instill in Joash is the same spark and love that He wants us to instill in others. It's a patient attitude, one where we understand that a real and loving relationship with God isn't going to be instantaneous but takes time and effort. And just as Joash must have seen God in Jehoiada, others must see God in our lives. Others should see Him in us because if they don't, all the "right" and "religious" words in the world won't make a bit of difference.

Jeremiah
Jeremiah 13:17

You know of him, of course. How could you miss a man who wrote two books of the Bible? And the books are long, two of the five included in the Major Prophet category. You probably know some of the conversations he had with God, especially when God told him, "I know the plans I have for you, plans to prosper you and not to harm you, plans to give you hope and a future."[7] You may even know that he was called the "weeping prophet." But what does that really mean? He cried a lot? What's so great about that? Everything.

Jeremiah was a man of tremendous passion, with a sincere heart that longed to please God. He was a man who looked out among his people every day and was heartbroken. He walked through Israel and saw a group of people that was no longer split between following God and Baals, but instead had clearly fallen away from the one true God.

Jeremiah, since the first chapter of his first book, speaks of an intimate relationship that he had with God, the very God who touched his lips and spoke through him. He knew that God was very real and wanted others to know that what came from his lips was straight from the mouth of God. But when he spoke, the people were unresponsive. The more he spoke, the less the people cared. They couldn't care about the God Jeremiah said was so near, because He seemed so far away. To them, God was nothing more than a grandmother's fairy tale. And it broke Jeremiah's heart.

No matter what he said, the people—God's own people—refused to listen. So Jeremiah would go home and just weep. "Why won't they listen? Why can't I make them understand who it is they're rejecting— that it's Him, not me. Why won't God make them listen?" The less they paid attention, the more he cried. The more they rejected, the less he could contain himself. He knew what they were missing, and his earnest desire was for them to know God. His desire was to do the will of the One who sent him, but his heart wasn't at peace knowing so many were lost.

Years later, the apostle Paul would echo Jeremiah's heart. In Acts 20:18–21, he said to the leaders of Ephesus, "You know how I lived the whole time I was with you . . . I served the Lord with great humility and with tears . . . You know that I have not hesitated to preach anything that would be helpful to you but have taught you publicly . . . I have declared to both Jews and Greeks that they must turn to God in repentance and have faith in our Lord Jesus." Paul spoke with tears, realizing not only the power of the message, but the great importance of the choice the people had to make. His heart was broken for the people.

And while the people in Jeremiah's day were pretty apathetic to God's message, he wasn't deterred. The more they rejected God, the more resolute he became in bringing God's message to the people. As badly as it hurt him to see them refuse to follow God, Jeremiah became more determined, not discouraged. The constant was his heart for people. He understood the message Jesus later would summarize as the greatest commandments. Love God, love people. And when they didn't love God back, he wept for them.

We should be exactly like Jeremiah in our passion to see people come to know Jesus Christ and have a relationship with Him. Those who reject Him shouldn't be scorned or rejected by us, but wept for because we clearly know that those who don't accept Christ are headed to hell. We can't accept Jesus for them, but we can pray for them. Our hearts should be broken for those who don't know Him because we know what they're missing. Understanding that they refuse a relationship with God shouldn't be more than we can bear. We must follow the example of Jeremiah to be firm in our purpose. We must continue to tell others about Him and show God off regardless of the attitude others show. We may not lead them to Christ, but we must never fail to try!

Gabriel
Luke 1:19

Gabriel is hard to miss, but easy to overlook. He had a critical role as one of God's angels and messengers. He was sent to the prophet Daniel to explain his vision, told Mary that she would be giving birth to the Messiah, and was sent to Zechariah to tell the old, faithful priest that he would be having a son despite his age.

But in this instance the surprise wasn't Gabriel's message as much as it was his response to Zechariah's question, "How can I be sure of this?"[8] Gabriel immediately answered Zechariah's question with, "I am Gabriel. I stand in the presence of God, and I have been sent to speak to you and to tell you this good news."[9]

Comedian Bill Cosby used to say that he would have to bargain with his children in order to watch the television shows that he wanted to watch. While watching *Gunsmoke*, his daughters wanted to watch *Froofie the Dog* and were trying to get him to change the channel for them. After realizing that a simple "No" wasn't going to work, Cosby said he felt like he had to show his own children his credentials as their father.[10] That must have been the same way that Gabriel felt about the situation with Zechariah. Here is an angel appearing before an old man who probably had never seen an angel before, and he dared to ask Gabriel what his qualifications were.

What a statement that Gabriel makes to Zechariah—and what thought must have been going through Zechariah's mind. Think of it—Gabriel literally stands before God. He spends his time in the very company of the One who spoke the universe into being. Gabriel's life is consumed by giving praise to and occasionally bringing the messages of Almighty God. What a life, to be consumed with God and to actually be in His midst, surrounded by His glory! Gabriel understood what we can only imagine—what Heaven is like, and what it is to be with God in the splendor of His holiness!

Think of it: Standing in the presence of God! Everything that is known about God, those things of His character that have been revealed to us, those glimpses of His glory that we're blessed with—all wrapped into one. And it's constant, not a glimpse or feeling, but an existence. Heaven will be non-stop with God, giving Him the praise that is due Him. One day, those who have a personal relationship with Jesus will understand that which Gabriel spoke of—an eternity in the presence of the Father.

Then Gabriel continued, saying that he was sent by God to deliver some very important and good news.

What it must have been like for Zechariah to hear the message! What it must have been like for Gabriel to deliver it! And what of Mary's message just a few verses later in Luke 1? What did it feel like, even for an angel, to be the one to speak those precious words to Mary that she would give birth to Jesus? Since the fall of man in the Garden of Eden, all of Heaven had been awaiting *the* moment—and Gabriel got to deliver the news. What a responsibility Gabriel had to deliver God's message!

That same message of good news has now been entrusted to us. Just as Gabriel came for the purpose of delivering God's message, we now have that same objective—to speak His words and share His heart with those who need to hear it. Usually we think of telling others the Gospel as a burden or a chore instead of realizing that we have the good news. We fail to realize that God, in some small way, treats us the same as the angels of Heaven. Proverbs 25:13 says, "Like the coolness of snow at harvest time is a trustworthy messenger to those who sent him; he refreshes the spirit of his masters." We have but one master, and we are to please Him. When God looked down on Gabriel, He must have been pleased with him. Hopefully, as God looks down on us, He feels the same way.

Simeon
Luke 2:25-35

The second chapter of Luke is one of the best-known chapters in the Bible. It doesn't have a designated title like Hebrews 11 (the Faith Chapter) or I Corinthians 13 (the Love Chapter), but it is where the Christmas story is found. And with so many important events, such as the birth of Jesus, or key figures, such as the angel and the shepherds, it's easy to overlook more minor characters. So often, the reading of the Christmas story is stopped at verse 20, and Simeon gets passed by.

Simeon is the man who was promised by God that he would not die until he saw the Messiah. That promise was fulfilled just eight days after the birth of Jesus, when Joseph and Mary took Him to the temple to be circumcised. Simeon was there solely because he was a godly man. Verse 25 describes Simeon as "righteous and devout." Here was a man who lived in a way that pleased God, and he was faithful despite the fact that God had been quiet now for 400 years. Simeon lived in an era when the Pharisees were teaching their own version of the Law, so it would have been easy to live more religious than right. But Simeon wasn't like that.

He was faithful and trusted God. Simeon is usually thought of as an old man who had been waiting for the fulfillment of the promise for a long time. Whether a long or short time, Simeon was faithful in waiting, and Luke doesn't give the impression that he was discouraged, however long it took. He trusted in God's promise without wavering. That's something that is difficult to do. Often when a promise from God is read or put on our hearts, we expect it to come to pass quickly.

When Moses was told by God that he would be sent to Egypt to speak to Pharaoh and lead the Israelites out, Moses went. He went to Pharaoh, spoke what God told him to speak, and then watched as Pharaoh ordered the slaves to make bricks without straw. The Israelites got mad at Moses, and Moses got mad at God. He questioned why God had sent him at all if this was how it was going to go. God had a plan. He wanted to show His power and would do that through the ten devastating plagues, proving that it was God and not man who freed the slaves. Simeon doesn't appear to question the promise of God. Whether it was weeks or decades, Simeon remained faithful to the Lord.

And then it happened. Simeon went to the temple, an action that seems so simple but tells us everything we need to know about him. "Moved by the Spirit, he went into the temple courts."[11] Simeon was in tune with the Holy Spirit and obedient when told where to go and what to do. It's the simple obedience of going into the temple courts that allowed him to see Jesus. Because Simeon was faithful and listened, he was able to hold the Messiah in his arms. There's no way of knowing what it must have been like for Simeon in those moments. The favorite Christmas song for many is *Mary Did You Know?*—one that wonders if Mary really understood exactly Who she was giving birth to. Simeon did know. He understood that he held salvation in his hands. What indescribable emotion Simeon must have experienced for those moments. And it was all made possible because he lived a life that pleased God and was obedient when led by the Spirit.

Who knows what kind of prompting that was for Simeon. Did he wonder why he was being led to the temple courts? Did he realize exactly how the day would unfold? Did he know what he was looking for? Even if he did, how many other baby boys were born on the same day that Jesus was? Simeon was rewarded because the Holy Spirit told him to go, and that was enough for him.

What an awesome thought to live a life that pleases God, to be faithful even during those days when we wonder if a promise will come to pass or not, to trust that God's timing and plan is perfect and that we can have complete confidence that the Holy Spirit has our best in mind. We can have assurance that no matter what happens, God is an honest and faithful Father. We understand that when we follow the lead of the Holy Spirit, the rewards can be truly amazing. Even if we've daydreamed about a situation, God's plan is so much greater than we ever could have anticipated! No matter what Simeon thought it would be like, it was no comparison to holding Jesus in his arms. What it must have been like to prophesy about the future of the Child whom he understood was the Messiah! And God has great things in store for us, too. All we have to do, like Simeon, is trust the Holy Spirit's leading and watch what happens.

Martha
Luke 10:38-42

Martha's doesn't have much of a role in the Gospels—in fact, she's always known in relation to someone else. She's Lazarus' sister, whose tears and sorrow over her brother's death actually prompted Jesus to weep. She's also Mary's sister, the one who was so busy in the kitchen and with the housework that she got mad at Mary for sitting at the feet of Jesus instead of joining her. Sure, Martha's easy to miss, just as easy as it is to miss the one who was sitting in her living room—Jesus.

You can picture Martha in the kitchen the day that Jesus was at their house. There was so much to be done. Frantically cooking and cleaning at the same time, she is trying to make sure that everything is just right. She's so preoccupied with her pursuit of the perfect evening that she barely notices the Essence of Perfection that sits in the next room. She walks through the room to get something and sees Mary sitting by Jesus.

Mary's gaze is so intense, she has forgotten about everything else. All she can comprehend are the words coming from Jesus' mouth—nothing else is important, including the cooking and cleaning that have consumed Martha. After all, it's Jesus that she's working for. She can *talk* to Him anytime, but now is the chance for her *to do* something for Him, and she's going to make the most of it. She's so focused on her tasks that she barely realizes Jesus is sitting there. All she sees is her lazy sister looking for an excuse to get out of her work.

Martha walks back into the kitchen, seething. She can't believe the attitude that her sister has. Martha stares at the meal and only sees what's wrong with it. Had Mary been helping the way she's supposed to, Martha would have been freed up to do other things. Anything wrong was Mary's fault. Martha tried to focus on her tasks, but couldn't. Now she was only focused on her lazy sister. And after a few more seconds of seeing red, Martha figured she would get some "divine intervention."

She went into the other room, hands on her hips and scowl on her face. She stared at the two of them for a second before blurting out, "Lord, don't you care that my sister has left me to do the work by myself? Tell her to help me!"[12] There, that would teach Mary. And Martha crossed her arms with a little smirk and waited for Jesus to scold her younger sister. Then Jesus calmly said, "Martha, Martha, you are worried and upset about many things, but only one thing is needed. Mary has chosen what is better . . ." Martha just stood there, stunned. Mary was right? How could she have picked the wrong thing—she was serving Him! Isn't that what He wanted?

It is—of course we're supposed to serve God, but in the right balance. If we become consumed with service for the Savior but forget the Savior we're serving, He can't be pleased. It's so easy to go about doing the Lord's work that we miss the Lord. Martha was so attentive to serving Jesus that she never spent any time with Him. And she missed out on the amazing blessings that Mary was receiving by sitting at the feet of Jesus. We tend to do the same thing in that we try to do God's work, getting so caught up and busy that we fail to spend time with God. And somehow we forget how crucial and important that time with God is. That's where we get our power—straight from the source. Without God, we become powerless and ineffective, no matter how much we do. Trying to do God's work without God is just aimless work!

Zacchaeus
Luke 19:1-10

All joking aside, it's pretty easy to miss the short man from the Gospels. With all the people that Jesus spoke to and performed miracles for, many of them seem to get lost in the crowd—which is exactly what Zacchaeus was so worried about. The irony is that instead of just being another body on the side of the road clamoring for a look at the very One who could be the Messiah, it turned out that Zacchaeus wasn't the one who was looking for someone special that day.

Zacchaeus lived in Jericho and made a good living as a tax collector. He made all his money, though at the risk of having an incredibly bad reputation. When word reached town that Jesus of Nazareth was coming through, Zacchaeus immediately wanted to see Him, but faced two main problems. The first one was obvious—he was at a height disadvantage and was worried that he wouldn't even get a peek at the man whom others said came from God. The second one was that being in a big crowd full of people that he had ripped off or cheated wasn't the most appealing thought.

So Zacchaeus looked around and noticed a sycamore fig tree that had some branches he could climb. He hurried over to the tree and started pulling his way up. The whole way up, Zacchaeus must have wondered what this Jesus of Nazareth looked like. Does He walk like a normal man or just float a couple inches off the ground like some mystical figure? Would he have light rays all around him? Once he finally got high enough, he turned back toward the road and waited for his glimpse of Jesus. Just as He came into view, Zacchaeus noticed something—He appeared to be looking right at him!

This couldn't be right. All these people, but it's as if Jesus' attention was focused on him. What's the deal? With all the people lining the street, why did this man's gaze seem to be coming back so often? Why was He so interested? What's He looking at, anyway? Zacchaeus may not have been sure how to feel until Jesus stopped—and spoke. "Zacchaeus, come down immediately. I must stay at your house today."[13] Was this really happening? Zacchaeus only climbed the tree to see Jesus, not entertain Him.

What Zacchaeus didn't know, of course, was that he didn't really climb the tree to see Jesus. He had climbed the tree because he was prompted by the Holy Spirit to do so. Jesus went to Jericho, in part, so He could introduce Himself to this crooked, morally deprived tax collector. The entire situation was orchestrated so that Jesus could clearly and obviously speak to Zacchaeus. So often, we read the story of Zacchaeus and mistakenly honor this "wee little man" for being the one who went to great lengths just to get a quick look at Jesus. The reality is that it's a snap shot of the heart of God—and Zaccheaus is a role player in the story, not the main character. It's not that Zaccheaus went out looking for Jesus, but that Jesus went to great lengths looking for one His lost sheep.

That's the way it's always been and always will be. We often get so caught up in thinking that we're "searching for God." The reality is that it's God who searches for us. It's God who created a universe that points us back to His glory. It was Jesus who humbled Himself and became a human just so we could see Him a little more clearly. God is the one who left His Word—an amazing love letter—which allows us to know Him and see Him for who He is. It is God's grand attempt to get the attention of His own creation, not us trying to find Him. If we to try and find God, where would we start? We have no concept or plan of going about it. Fortunately, God seeks us out and puts us in position to clearly see Him. He invited Himself into Zaccheaus' house, just as He invites Himself into our hearts. The rest of it, our response to Him, is up to us.

Stones
Luke 19:40

What? Stones? Yes—and not the Rolling ones, either. Jesus spoke about them. And they would have spoken back, if they had the chance. It's simple to miss because Jesus referenced them in just one verse. Oh—and they're stones! Think about the last time you paid any attention to a stone—not including the random one that hits your windshield on the highway. But taking a closer look at them, as Jesus spoke of them, they play an amazing role.

The scene is classic: Jesus is riding into Jerusalem on a colt just six days before He would be crucified. Jesus is the focus of everyone's attention and praise. As he goes down the road, people are flocking for a glimpse at Him. Others are taking off their cloaks and gently placing them on the dirt path, the way they would for royalty. Followers are caught up in the moment and begin quoting Scripture in praise of their Master.

"Blessed is the king who comes in the name of the Lord!" and "Peace in Heaven and glory in the highest."[14] These are some of the greatest praises that they could give the one Who so deserves adoration. The Pharisees, never far behind when Jesus was the focus of attention, are furious. They never could understand why so many people loved and put their faith in this man, and this was too much! They cannot sit back and listen to a man being inappropriately praised. And this wasn't any man—this is Jesus, the one who has openly challenged what they taught and their sincerity. This false prophet cannot mislead the people, so the Pharisees speak up. As Jesus passes by, a group of them shout out, "Teacher, rebuke your disciples!"[15]

Jesus looked at them with great intensity. He knew they would not accept Him—He knew, since He formed them in their mothers' wombs. He'd known they would reject and misunderstand Him even before His Father began creating the universe. And yet it must have broken His heart the way that they treated Him. In His humanity, He must have wondered how those who knew the scriptures best were the ones who never realized who He was. And now they wanted to silence the few that were giving Him the praise that He deserved. So He simply responded, "I tell you, if they keep quiet, the stones will cry out."[16]

What a thought! Whoever wrote Psalm 148 reminds us that all things above the earth and below it need to praise the Lord. But all of those things are living creations. Had Jesus said that the grass would cry out, it would have made a little more sense since grass is a living thing. If He had said that the trees or birds would proclaim His praise, we could understand it a little. But a stone—it's a completely inanimate object that has no ability to speak or do anything of the sort—according to our knowledge.

Imagine what it would have been like if no one had spoken that day! The stones would have been compelled to sing the praise of their Creator, just like the angels in Isaiah 6. The Heavens declare the glory of God every second. Whenever He looks down at His amazingly vast creation, it worships Him. The rocks wanted their chance, too. Unfortunately, they wouldn't get it this day.

Of all the things that have been made, man, the most prized of creation, is the one that has been given the option of worshiping Him—for now. But with so many forms of worship, we still often fail to praise our King. All of the celestial beings shout of God's glory. The oceans praise His might. Everything from the setting of the sun to the wind blowing through the trees is a form of worship and adoration of the King.

And then there are humans. We're the creation that lets Him down the most. We're the ones who reject and shame Him. We're the ones that are so caught up with ourselves that we fail to notice Him. We even killed Him when He came to reveal Himself to us. Let's not make the mistake that so many others have made. We need to have the same urgency that the stones have. Let's keep them silent and give the Glorious One the adoration He so deserves. It's an honor to be in the presence of holiness and proclaim His majesty—don't give it up to a bunch of stones!

Andrew
John 1:35-42

Andrew—we know his name and his role, but not much else. Usually we consider him only as Peter's brother, who also followed Jesus, when actually the opposite is quite true. Andrew was the trendsetter—the first one to follow Jesus after John the Baptist proclaimed, "Look, the Lamb of God." And after an introduction like that, how could Andrew think about doing anything but getting to know this man who appeared to be human like everyone else. Andrew, however, must have instinctively realized there was something more.

Andrew first followed John, realizing than he was more that just some crazy, locust-chomping, repent-spewing, Pharisee-convicting man who liked to baptize people in the Jordan River. He understood that John was a prophet who was preparing the way for Jesus. That's why Andrew followed John and learned from him, which is what made him more inclined to follow the man that John bowed down to. Chances are that Andrew was there when John said that he wasn't even worthy to untie Jesus' sandals and there at the baptism when people saw Jesus exalted by the heavens and heard Him being praised by God Himself. Andrew had to know that there was something very different about Jesus.

So Andrew followed Jesus that first day, not knowing where he was being led or why. He spent an entire day with Jesus, hearing, literally, from the mouth of God. What did they talk about? Did Andrew actually understand Who it was that was speaking to him? He must have, because verses 41–42 say, "The first thing Andrew did was to find his brother Simon and tell him, 'We have found the Messiah' . . . And he brought him to Jesus."

"The first thing Andrew did . . ." signifies that no matter what else was going on, it was pressing on his heart so much that he had to find Peter. Charlie Peace, a thief in England, was on his way to the gallows when an Anglican priest read that those who die without Christ are headed for a painful eternity in hell. Charlie turned around and asked the priest if he believed what he had just read. The priest, caught off guard, answered with a less-than-inspiring "Yes." Charlie then said, "Well I don't. But if I did, I'd get down on my hands and knees and crawl all over Great Britain, even if it were paved with pieces of broken glass, if I could just rescue one person from what you just told me."[17] Andrew had a heart like that. One that was so burdened with the good news of meeting Jesus that he was compelled to tell Peter.

John went on to write that Andrew went and found Peter, which implies that there was some sort of search involved. Andrew wasn't deterred if Peter wasn't in the first place that he looked or that he had to do some work. Andrew had met the Messiah, and there would be no alternative but to find his brother and hope that he had a similar experience.

Finally, Andrew brought Peter to Jesus. It was a physical thing—not that Peter was dragged, but probably that Andrew was such a salesman that Peter wanted to know who this Jesus was. Peter could see the excitement in his brother's eyes and hear it in Andrew's voice. It was a passion that could not be deterred. It was contagious, and Peter wanted to meet this man—the one who would eventually change Peter's life in numerous ways!

Andrew was the first one to witness. Just as the Samaritan woman at the well was the vehicle that God used to reach so many other Samaritans, Andrew was the one that was used to bring Peter. What if Andrew hadn't told his brother and wanted Jesus for himself, or was so afraid of what other people thought that he said nothing? How different would the start of the church, the day of Pentecost, and the lives of so many be if Andrew had kept quiet or allowed himself to be discouraged? We need to have the same passion that Andrew had about reaching those who don't know Jesus. If you know Him, you should be excited about Him and actively search for others to bring to Him.

Royal Official
John 4:46-54

How much faith do you think you have? A lot? A little? None? We sing about it, talk about it, and pray for it. But faith isn't something you proclaim, it's something you exercise. And the only way to know how much faith you have is to be put in a situation where you have to use it. Take the royal official, for example. He traveled a great distance to see Jesus and beg Him for help. His son lay sick at home, moments from death, and he realized that Jesus was his son's only hope. So he went to speak with Jesus, but the response that the official received had to be less than expected.

The official obviously had faith in Jesus. He went approximately 20 miles from his home in Capernaum to Cana, where Jesus was visiting. No man, regardless of need, would go that far—possibly on foot—unless he believed the person at the end of the journey could be of assistance. But this man had heard of Jesus, maybe even seen a miracle or heard some of his teaching, and knew there was something completely different about Him. He may have understood that Jesus was, in fact, more than mere man because he called Jesus, "Sir."[18] Here was an official, probably one of King Herod's top guys, lowering himself to less than the stature of a Jew. It wasn't that he'd forgotten his place in the empire, but he grasped his role in eternity. The official bowed down before the true King, not just because he could heal his son, but also because Jesus was so deserving of his praise—even though he was so unworthy to give it.

The official had a couple of expectations of Jesus, and the first one was clearly that He would go to the sick boy. To this point, Jesus had always been at the place where His miracles had occurred. Either He'd touched the people or spoken to them. Even when the water was turned to wine, Jesus was at the wedding feast. So the official arrived, found Jesus, and asked him to come to back to his house and heal his son. Then Jesus gave him the response that must have caught the official off guard. "You may go. Your son will live."[19]

"You may go?" The official must have wondered if he'd heard Jesus right. Seriously, leave and go home? But how would Jesus heal the boy if He didn't go with him? The official expected one response and got a totally different one. After traveling 20 miles to get Jesus to heal his son, he was supposed to turn around and go home empty-handed with some promise that he would live? What if it didn't take and Jesus had to be there to fix it? This wasn't the way it was supposed to go!

And then it happened—the official turned around and went home. His son was still at home, and Jesus wasn't going to go with him—and the official still left. That is similar to the acts of faith that earned men such as Noah and Abraham a place in Hebrews 11, basically the Old Testament Hall of Fame. Noah built a giant boat for animals, even though he lived in the desert and had never seen rain before. Abraham was told to go to a land he didn't know about with a promise of future success. Both men were obedient and faithful and rewarded for it. The same is true for the royal official, who was told to go home and his son would live. He had the faith to leave. Would you have been able to turn around and go home if a loved one lay sick?

On his way home, the official was met by his servants. They told him the good news that Jesus' words were as true as he'd hoped and that his son was no longer sick. Understandably, the first thing the official asked his servants was when it was that the boy had been healed. They told him the time—the exact same time that Jesus said the words, " . . . your son will live." And once again, Jesus proves the point—He is completely trustworthy, and we can put our faith in Him.

The royal official demonstrates a faith that is nearly unfathomable. He showed us that regardless of who we are in the world's eyes, we must be completely humble before the Creator of the world. The official shows us that our plans and God's aren't always going to be the same, but that we should trust Him—because He is, in fact, faithful. His love and provision know no end, unless we don't have the faith that allows for miracles to happen. We need to be willing to submit to His plans and release our own, realizing that faith in Him provides us with amazing blessings.

Boy
John 6:9

It's pretty easy to miss him. No name, no identity other than the fact that he was a male under the age of 13. The only other notable thing about him is simply that he was the catalyst for one of Jesus' most impressive miracles—at least from a pure numbers standpoint. Because of this boy's unselfishness and Jesus' proving that He can use anyone who simply wants to be used, thousands of hungry people were fed.

The story is well-known. Jesus was on a mountainside spending time with His disciples when a crowd of people came to hear Him speak—thousands of people—including 5,000 men who hungered to hear Jesus teach and to be healed by Him. Instead of sending them away so He could be alone with the disciples, Jesus had compassion on the crowds and embraced them. So they stayed. And stayed. And stayed.

Before anyone knew it, it was getting late, and the people were getting hungry. Jesus asked Phillip, who was from nearby Bethsaida, where they could get food for the people. It was something of a trick question because John notes that Jesus already knew what He was planning to do. But Phillip didn't get it; he told Jesus there was no way they could get enough money to feed so many hungry people. Then Andrew came over and had a boy with him, a boy who had five barley loaves, two fish—and a servant's heart. And those seven pieces of food were more than enough for Jesus to feed everyone.

The boy is impressive for a couple of reasons. First, he volunteered himself. It's hard to imagine that 12 disciples would be urgently searching through a crowd of thousands for scraps of food—especially because Jesus had just brought the matter to Phillip's attention. Instead, the boy probably took a quick look at the situation, saw that no one around him had any food, noticed that the guys with Jesus were looking panicked, and then realized that he could fill a need.

Second, the boy gave everything that he had when no one else would. Do you really think that no one else out of thousands of people had any food, or that this one boy's mother was the only one in the area who thought ahead that he might get hungry? Five thousand men and their families in the crowd, and only one of them packed a snack? That's highly unlikely. Maybe the disciples themselves had food with them but figured that the meager portions they had were in no way enough for all those people. They were so focused on their own understanding that they forgot about the one Who goes beyond our limits. And so they offered nothing. But the boy held nothing back—and he would have been justified to keep a little for himself. No one would have faulted him for asking for say, enough food to make a small fish sandwich. Instead, he gave Jesus everything he had.

It's the same as the widow, who put just two copper coins in the offering.[20] Although those coins are only worth a fraction of a penny, Jesus told his disciples that she was the one who gave the most because she gave all that she had. Paul reminded the people of Corinth of the same thing, saying, "Each man should give what he has decided in his heart to give, not reluctantly or under compulsion, for God loves a cheerful giver. And God is able to make all grace abound to you, so that in all things at all times, having all that you need, you will abound in every good work."[21]

How true this statement is when you think of the boy who gave his lunch to Jesus. He gave what he could, not because one of the disciples forced him to or because Jesus expected him to, but because he wanted to. And because of it, God provided everything that he needed. Not only for the boy or whatever members of the boy's family that may have been there, but for everyone. All the people were blessed because of the boy's willingness to give.

There's a lot to be learned from this unnamed child. Maybe it's to have a child-like faith, trusting God with everything we have without thinking of how little it may be. We should understand that just because it seems like little to us doesn't mean that God can't multiply it exponentially. We need to understand that God can't be put in a box, because we know that there's nothing that limits Him. If people who claimed to be followers of Jesus would fill needs that they see and give to a trustworthy God, how different would the world be?

Pharisees
John 8:1-9

The Pharisees get more than their 15 minutes of fame in the Bible, so it's nearly impossible to miss them. So why include them? Because we definitely do miss their significant role in the story. We remember the adulterous woman who was thrown at Jesus feet. We look at the response of Jesus, who was amazingly cool as the Pharisees attempted to incriminate Him. And we know that the Pharisees left in shame, but there's a major story in between.

This was the moment that the ultra-zealous Pharisees had been waiting for. How it exactly happened, we don't know. Did they catch the woman in the act? It probably wasn't that hard to find a prostitute—if she was that—working while there was a festival in Jerusalem. But they practically had to find her in the act in order to be able to honestly accuse her. In their zeal, however, they failed to follow the letter of the Law. Instead of bringing both the man and woman to be stoned, as Leviticus 20 stated, they only brought the woman, whom you can imagine being shamefully clothed at the time, and marched her through the temple courts toward Jesus.

Unfortunately, this is a very proud time for the Pharisees. They have no concern for the woman they're condemning to death. She's nothing more than a pawn in the real life game of cat-and-mouse they're trying to play with Jesus. They take great satisfaction in this—walking through the temple courtyard with everyone looking at them. Whatever they can do to take attention off Jesus—and back onto themselves—was a positive for them. As they approach Jesus, almost nothing could take the smug looks off their faces.

By the time they reach Jesus, the crowd is completely focused on them. They shove the woman in front of Jesus, almost forming a semi-circle around her. From above, it must look like a schoolyard brawl is about to break out with the Pharisees on one side, Jesus on the other, and a scared woman in the middle. She knows that death is coming.

The Pharisees quickly state their case and wait for Jesus to say something—anything that they can arrest Him for. This is the perfect spot: there are so many witnesses to hear whatever Jesus will say. Once they're done speaking, the silence is almost eerie. The Pharisees are quietly rejoicing; Jesus is just quiet. The longer Jesus goes without speaking, the more confident the Pharisees get. Jesus bends down, still not speaking. As the Pharisees would later realize again during Jesus' trial, sometimes His silence is as disarming as His words. He writes something in the sand.

The Pharisees, refusing to be ignored, continue to

pepper Jesus with questions. His silence has caused them to be downright indignant. Their tone changes from supremely righteous to completely spiteful. The focus of their questions is starting to move from the woman to Jesus. Still saying nothing, He just writes in the sand. They're oblivious to His words—they always were. Jesus stands up, flicks the sand off His finger, and looks at the woman's accusers. Finally, He's going to speak. The crowd is completely still. One wrong word from Jesus would be an instant death sentence, and everyone knows it. Without a trace of fear or contempt, He says, "If any one of you is without sin, let him be the first to throw a stone at her."[22] He waits a second to let His words sink in before bending down and writing in the sand again.

Like watching two people argue, the crowd collectively turns their heads away from Jesus and toward the Pharisees. The Pharisees look at each other. What do they do now? Jesus just put the onus on them. The woman closes her eyes and cringes, believing she'll be crushed by stones at any second. None of the Pharisees say a word. Intuitively, each one looks to the oldest of the group. He is the wisest and most experienced and will know what to do. The look on his face is both upset and humiliated. He stops looking at Jesus, then looks down. He studies the ground for a few seconds, slowly taking a few steps backward and walking away.

The whole time, Jesus never looks up. With one sentence, this dream situation had become a nightmare. One-by-one, the Pharisees leave. The crowd is still silent, except for the few gasps when they see their religious leaders publicly shamed.

Sadly, we recreate this scene with God all too often. We've all had those moments when we question the justice and decisions of our Heavenly Father. We convince ourselves that the God who claims to be holy and almighty has somehow dropped the ball. In spite, we throw someone else before His throne. Someone who we believe isn't living as righteously as we think we are. Someone who doesn't deserve God's favor but is receiving it anyway. And that doesn't meet our approval. Somehow we're trying to make the One without sin feel guilty. In those moments, as we try to shame someone—and God in the process—we highlight our own shortcomings. With complete silence, the God we've attempted to humiliate turns the tables on us. And in the presence of holiness, we realize how insignificant we are. Like the Pharisees, we try to leave with our heads down. Unlike the Pharisees, though, the invisible hand of a loving and forgiving Father stops us. And hopefully, we then fall on our face in His presence.

Philip
Acts 8:26-40

Philip's a guy we know a little information about but tend to overlook at the same time. He was one of Jesus' disciples, but wasn't one of the "big three," these being Peter, James, and John. He was in the room on the Day of Pentecost when the Holy Spirit came upon them. He was living in Jerusalem until Stephen's death and then left the city as so many other believers did. And just as those who scattered spread the Gospel wherever they went, Philip did the same. Actually, his first stop was a city in Samaria. He brought the Gospel to the same people that the Jews had despised, but Jesus had loved. Philip didn't do many amazing things, but he did do what the Holy Spirit told him to do. More importantly, Philip had an amazing attitude doing it. Some are willing to do God's will; Philip was thrilled about it.

One of Philip's greatest qualities was that he mimicked many of the traits that his teacher had. Philip's desire when he appears in the book of Acts was to be desire-less, literally doing only the will of the One who sent him. He received no glory for himself, sometimes leaving the scene before someone could wrongly praise him instead of his Master. Philip knew the Old Testament and was able to clearly explain it to others . . . maybe because the One he followed for three years was both the personification and fulfillment of the Word.

When an angel told Philip to "go south to the road—the desert road—that goes down from Jerusalem to Gaza,"[23] Philip went. With the faith that Abraham displayed, Philip went without asking why. Things were going very well in Samaria. The good news was being preached, evil spirits were being cast out, people were being healed, and the city was pleased. Leaving may not have made sense, but Philip was undeterred. Although he had no idea what awaited him on the road, he realized that at the very least he would have the opportunity to be used by God.

As he walked, he saw a chariot going along the road. Either Philip was walking quickly, the chariot driver was moving slowly, or God just wanted to make sure they met up. In the back of the chariot, an Ethiopian official was reading what appeared to be a scroll. The closer Philip got, the more excited he became. By the time the Spirit quietly said, "Go to that chariot and stay near it,"[24] Philip could barely contain himself.

Philip didn't just walk to the chariot, he ran. Nothing would stop him, and nothing could be more urgent. This could be greater than life or death—it was an eternal matter. Philip raced down the road at such a speed that it felt like his legs might give out underneath him. We don't know how far he ran—it could have been a few yards or half a mile. But just as Elijah ran down Mt. Carmel, Philip ran at an amazing pace—fueled from above.

When he got to the chariot, Philip could overhear the man reading aloud. He clearly recognized the words of the prophet Isaiah. Without any further prompting, Philip asked the man if he understood what he was reading. Within seconds, Philip was in the chariot with the man. It might have been one of the situations where he needed to catch himself and slow himself down because he was so excited.

We could use an attitude like Philip's. One where we're so excited to be used by the King of Kings that we literally run at the chance. But we usually take an opposite attitude. We have so many things on our schedule that adding anything—even if it is for God's glory—is just a burden. When we see something or someone in our way, we tend to see an obstacle instead of a divine opportunity. Then again, we often aren't even quiet enough to be steered in the right direction. Sometimes we need to just slow down and open our eyes. We need to be willing, even hungry, for the chance to be used by God and bring glory to Him. Because it's bigger than life or death—it's an eternal matter.

Believers in Antioch
Acts 11:19-26

It's easy to miss the ones who were first called *Christians*, since Luke adds that sentence in as a footnote at the end of verse 26. Almost casually, he says, "The disciples were called *Christians* first at Antioch." But to think about how differently that word is used *now* makes us understand how important the term was *then*. Jesus Christ—the very name induced outrage, and to follow His teachings was to take your life into your own hands. You want to be a believer? You may as well sign up for the death sentence. And to be called a Christian was both extremely frightening and completely exhilarating.

Let's back up. The believers wound up in Antioch out of necessity. Once Stephen was stoned, staying in Jerusalem was the last thing people wanted to do. If they didn't leave after Stephen died, they fled soon, as Saul started to go on the prowl. So they scattered all over the Roman Empire. Instead of keeping to themselves the Gospel that could get them killed, they spread it everywhere they went. It was something that they just couldn't hold in. They knew the consequences if they told the wrong person, but it was more than worth the risk.

At first, the message was told only to the Jews. After

all, Jesus was a Jew, and He was their promised Messiah. Then the believers in Antioch stepped way out and started telling the Greeks. By doing this, they not only risked upsetting other believers, they also fulfilled what the angel said to the shepherds when Jesus' birth was announced: "I bring you good news of great joy that will be for *all* the people"[25] (emphasis added).

News of the church at Antioch spread because of the way the Gospel had spread. A great number of people were being saved and changing their lives, and that's a difficult thing to keep quiet. When Barnabas arrived and encouraged them, even more began following Christ. Then Barnabas went looking for Saul, the same man who indirectly caused the Gospel to spread by trying to kill those who believed it. When Saul (whose name is later changed to Paul) arrived, he and Barnabas had a year's worth of training and teaching to do, because there were so many that were hungry for the Word.

And then someone said it, and it probably wasn't one of the believers. It's doubtful that they were seeking a group name. Chances are it was someone who said it in conversation about a believer.

"Oh, did you hear about her? She's been with all those fanatics."

"Yes, but her life is so different."

"You've noticed that too! They all seem 'changed,'

if that's possible. I have another friend who believed, too. They're just changing, every day."

"What is it they believe in?"

"I hear it's the teachings of . . . Jesus."

"The one who was crucified a few years ago! You know, I saw him once. He touched this man who couldn't walk, and the man literally jumped up! And the way he talked, firm but loving, you know?"

"Loving—that's it! She's been more loving than before. It's like she's acting the way that Jesus did."

"Yeah, they're all like Him now."

"They killed the one claiming to be the Christ, but we've got a whole bunch of little Christ's running around. A bunch of . . . Christians."

Christian—ask 30 people today what it means and listen to 29½ answers. Whether it's Christ-like, little Christ, or follower of Christ, the bottom line is that it is someone who acts like Jesus. It's that person who patterns their life after Jesus in every way and tries to mirror His heart. Even James said that actions are key. "What good is it, my brothers, if a man claims to have faith but has deeds? . . . In the same way, faith by itself, if it is not accompanied by action, is dead."[26]

Imagine what it was like for those early believers to be called Christians. To hear that others thought they were like Christ! What an honor! What a fallacy! Obviously they fell short, but they did their absolute best to act like Him, to mirror and obey his teaching, and others could see that clearly. Thus they called them Christians. It was a deserved honor. We usually do the opposite: We call someone a Christian based solely on a decision to accept Jesus and hope that their actions don't shame His name. We have it backwards. Once we find our identity in Christ, our actions should back it up. Don't claim it and then hope for the best; live it out and then earn the title.

Silas
Acts 16:16-40

They say you never get a second chance to make a first impression, and Silas made sure that his first encounters with people made lasting memories. Silas is one of the many amazing men Luke wrote about in the book of Acts, which makes it simple to overlook some of them. But Silas is one of those who served God wherever he was and never wavered in his faith despite going through difficult times. No matter what happened to Silas, he was unyielding in his love and reverence for God.

The first time he's mentioned is in Acts 15, when the church council is prompted to send Judas and Silas to Paul and Barnabas in Antioch. Silas wasn't in Antioch for long, but strengthened the church and the believers there. Whatever he did, he must have been supremely focused on serving God and the believers there because Paul was impressed. So much so that when he and Barnabas argued and split at the end of chapter 15, Silas was the one that Paul chose to accompany him. As we read it now, we imagine the kind of thrill this must have been for Silas—going on a journey with Paul, the man that God used to spread the gospel to so many people. But for Silas, it probably wasn't about Paul. He wasn't a best-selling author, just one chosen by God to bring the good news. And Silas was being sent out to do the same.

When Silas and Paul made a stop in Philippi, a demon-possessed girl harassed them. The minute Paul commanded the spirit to leave her, Silas probably knew that something bad was about to happen. After all, this girl had made her owners a lot of money, and now her ability to predict the future was gone. Sure enough, her owners lashed out at them—literally. Within minutes, he and Paul were standing before an angry mob in the marketplace. The magistrates found themselves in a situation very similar to Pilate when Jesus was on trial and decided to have Paul and Silas sent to jail. It's better to wrongly accuse a few men than to have hundreds of angry people on your hands.

Silas may never have been persecuted before, but as they tied his hands to the post, he understood exactly what he was about to endure. He closed his eyes and braced for the first blow. The whip caught him just under the shoulder, and the sting was unbearable. He could feel the skin opening, blood trickling down his back. Just as he started to adjust to that feeling, it came down again. And again. And again. He wasn't just flogged, the beating was severe. They dragged him inside the jail and dropped his limp body on the hard floor. He was almost completely unconscious when he felt the steel shackles attached to his feet.

When he opened his eyes, Silas took a few moments to realize where he was. He didn't know if he'd been out for minutes or hours, but he quickly remembered the beating. With each subtle movement of his body, his back screamed out. He wasn't sure what to do. He slowly moved his head to the left and saw Paul. He wasn't in any better shape. One asked the other if he was alright. The other let out a frustrated snicker, both realizing how pointless the question was. Quietly, Paul started to pray. He wasn't venting to God, but rather praying for the people who had just beaten him.

Silas sat stunned for a second before joining in. What started out as a whisper got louder and louder. The more they prayed, the less they felt the pain from the whipping. The longer he prayed, Silas became overwhelmed. He remembered the words of Jesus when he said, "Blessed are you when people insult you, persecute you and falsely say all kinds of evil against you because of me. Rejoice and be glad because great is your reward in heaven . . ."[27] Silas repeated these words to Paul a few times before they began to sing songs of praise. What an honor to be persecuted for the Lord! And they thanked Him for it.

As they sang, it was as if the floor began to shaking. No wait, it really was. One of the other prisoners shouted "Earthquake!" just as the shackles around Silas' ankles snapped. The quake was over within seconds, but it was strong enough that all the cell doors were opened. In the quiet, Silas could hear the noise of metal quickly sliding from its sheath. Paul, realizing that the jailer was about to kill himself, shouted out that everyone was still in their cells. Within seconds, the jailer was on the floor on his knees before Paul and Silas asking what he must do to be saved. Their first impression left no doubt Who it was they followed, and the jailer wanted to follow the same One.

How do you react when tough times come? Your responses are a true barometer for the type of impression you're making on others. Are you like Job, who fell to his knees in worship when he was at his lowest point? Or are you like Job's wife, who advised her husband to curse God? Being able to hold to an unwavering faith can point others around you closer to the Savior. Silas did that, and many others were saved because of his passion for the Lord. Wouldn't it be great to have that be true in your life?

(Endnotes)

1   Genesis 24:14

2   John C. Maxwell, *Running With The Giants*
(Warner Books, 2002)

3   I Samuel 14:7

4   II Kings 22:8

5   II Kings 22:10

6   II Timothy 3:16

7   Jeremiah 29:11

8   Luke 1:18

9   Luke 1:19

10   Bill Cosby, *Bill Cosby at His Best*
(MCA Special Products, 1995)

11   Luke 2:27

12   Luke 10:40

13   Luke 19:5

14   Luke 19:38

15   Luke 19:39

16   Luke 19:40

17   Tony Campolo, *Let Me Tell You a Story*
(W Publishing Group, 2000)

18   John 4:49

19   John 4:50

TATE PUBLISHING *& Enterprises*

Tate Publishing is committed to excellence in the publishing industry. Our staff of highly trained professionals, including editors, graphic designers, and marketing personnel, work together to produce the very finest books available. The company reflects the philosophy established by the founders, based on Psalms 68:11,

"THE LORD GAVE THE WORD AND GREAT WAS THE COM-
PANY OF THOSE WHO PUBLISHED IT."

If you would like further information, please call
1.888.361.9473
or visit our website
www.tatepublishing.com

TATE PUBLISHING *& Enterprises*, LLC
127 E. Trade Center Terrace
Mustang, Oklahoma 73064 USA